JEFF TOGHILL

Learning to Sail

M000043152

W · W · NORTON & COMPANY
New York · London

Library of Congress Cataloging-in-Publication Data
Toghill, Jeff E.
  Learning to sail.
  1. Sailing. I. Title.
GV811.T55   1986   797.1'24   85–18830

ISBN 0-393-30298-9

W. W. Norton & Company, Inc., 500 Fifth Avenue, New York, N.Y. 10110
W. W. Norton & Company Ltd., 37 Great Russell Street, London WC1B 3NU

1 2 3 4 5 6 7 8 9 0

Contents

Introduction

Man is born with an insatiable competitive urge. It first surfaces in childhood squabbles over possession of some trivia, and is fostered and encouraged through youthful development in school, on the playing fields and in leisure activities. It flowers into maturity in business or in adult sport where it can be given full rein.

In the early days, sailing was a means of carrying on trade and the only aspect of competition involved was in getting to the markets first. Perhaps unwittingly, this created some of the finest competitive sailing ever seen and ever likely to be seen, as giant clippers thundered across the oceans at speeds up to 20 knots. Such feats have never been repeated, even with the advent of modern technology and the development of sailing as a professional sport. It was a heyday of competitive sailing even though the catalyst was purely commercial with little thought given to pride of achievement or the stimulation and satisfaction of successfully challenging the elements.

Since that early time, sailing has become a classic sport and has developed through the ages to the billion dollar activity that it is today. But while increasing millions of dollars are spent every year in the sailing arena, paradoxically it has become less and less a wealthy man's sport. Today, anyone can enjoy the thrills and the spills, and kids are taught sailing as part of their school curriculum. It is a sport for all ages. An open, uninhibited sport where cares and pressures are blown away by the challenge of the wind and waves.

Like all professionals, I believe that sailing is a sport that cannot be successfully learned from a book. But when practical tuition is not available, and since, in any case, a book provides a useful backup when practical tuition is available, it seemed a worthwhile challenge to attempt to disprove my own theory and attempt to write a book from which sailing **could** be learned.

To keep as close as possible to practical tuition, I decided to use the visual approach, using my camera as much as, if not more than, my typewriter.

The initial results, published in one of my

earlier books, seemed to achieve the desired effect. The technique has been refined in this series of training booklets to the point where the advantages of practical tuition have been achieved as nearly as possible in print.

This booklet, like the others in the series, introduces sailing to those of any age who have not as yet, 'sniffed the wind'.

Parts of a small sailing boat

1. Bow (or stem)
2. Transom (or stern)
3. Beam (starboard side)
4. Gunwale (port side)
5. Chainplates (with shrouds attached)
6. Rudder
7. Centreboard (in casing)
8. Thwarts (or seats)
9. Tiller (with extension)
10. Spars (boom right, spinnaker pole left)
11. Mast step

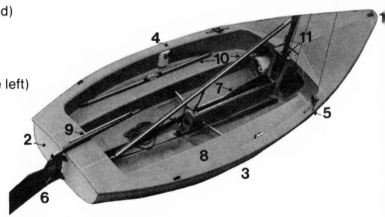

Parts of the rig

1. Jib (or headsail)
2. Mainsail
3. Peak (or Head) of sail
4. Clew (of mainsail)
5. Tack (of headsail)
6. Shroud
7. Mainsheet tackle
8. Jib sheeting track
9. Luff (of headsail)
10. Leech (of mainsail with battens inserted)
11. Jib halyard

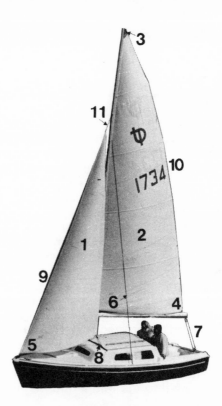

Sailing clothing

It is important to wear the right clothing when sailing, otherwise what should be an enjoyable and exciting sport can turn out to be most uncomfortable, even hazardous occupation. It is always colder on the water than you might expect. One reason is that you are in the open, away from the warm, sun-heated land and therefore subject to the full bite of the sea-cooled wind. And there is always spray or some other form of moisture flying around which, unless you are properly protected, will soak your clothes and cause a drop in body temperature.

Even in the warmest climates, prolonged exposure to conditions such as these can cause discomfort or even mild hypothermia. In colder climates sailing can be a dangerous sport if the correct clothing is not worn. Evaporation of moisture from the body surfaces follows the basic principles on which refrigerators are designed, and it is not hard to imagine that if the body is subjected to the temperatures inside a refrigerator, it will not only fail to function properly but may not function at all!

In warm climates the sun can be as hazardous as the cold and a peaked cap, adequate skin covering and sunglasses are essential. Protective lotions and creams must also be used to protect the exposed areas of skin from the sun's damaging rays.

1. Neoprene wetsuits are essential where the air temperature is low or where the skin is constantly saturated.
2. Good wet weather suits must fit well around neck and sleeves to prevent water seeping in during long sailing sessions. Heavy weather suits are ideal for cold conditions, but tend to get steamy in mild or warm weather.
3. Lightweight jackets are more suited to dinghy and catamaran sailing as the heavier offshore gear tends to be cumbersome in the more active environment of small boats.

Personal buoyancy

No matter how good a sailor you are, sooner or later you will 'pickle' the boat—capsize it—and find yourself in the water. This is no great problem, indeed it is a part of sailing small boats. But it is very important that when it does happen you are prepared for it. And the most essential form of preparation is to be wearing the right buoyancy equipment.

Even the best swimmer can tire quickly when trying to right a capsized boat. Similarly, if for some reason you have to swim for it, the shore is always farther away than you think. Other problems can also arise at times like this and to be without some form of support in the water is to court disaster.

Unfortunately, most life-jackets are by their nature cumbersome and ill-suited for use in small craft, so a compromise must be reached whereby the maximum support can be gained with the least cumbersome equipment. The best approach is to first learn to swim, at which point you can use the far more comfortable buoyancy vest or approved inflatable vests rather than the bulky, full support life-jackets.

All personal buoyancy gear is graded according to body weight, and all must meet the required standard laid down by the Standards Association.

1. Effective, but very cumbersome, life-jackets known as the MOT type, are difficult to wear in small sailboats. It is virtually impossible for someone in the water to scramble back aboard a boat when wearing one of these.
2. More suitable, tailored life-jackets still provide full support but are less cumbersome than other types. However, they still tend to inhibit the fast mobility which is essential when hiking out in a stiff breeze in a small sailboat.
3. More compact, comfortable buoyancy vests permit almost unrestricted activity, but do not provide full support in the water. Providing you can swim, these are adequate for small boat sailing.

Rigging the boat

Keel yachts have their masts and rigging permanently in place and therefore need only to have the sails bent on and they are ready for sailing. Trailerable yachts, centreboarders and catamarans, by contrast, must be totally portable and thus have mast, spars and rigging which can be taken down and stowed when the boat is not in use. Before these boats are ready to sail, they must first be rigged by erecting the mast and securing the rigging and fittings as well as bending on the sails.

The rigging procedure will vary according to the type of boat. 'Cat' rigged craft such as the Laser have no standing rigging and the sail is sleeved onto the mast. Other centreboarders and catamarans have shrouds and stays and the sail is set into a groove on the mast. A basic outline of both types of craft is given here, although the illustrations are of a Laser.

1. Sort out the mast and rigging (if any) and lay the mast along the boat with the foot of the mast in position near the mast step. In the case of unstayed masts, the sail should now be sleeved onto the mast. Where rigging is involved, the shrouds should be connected to the chainplates.

①

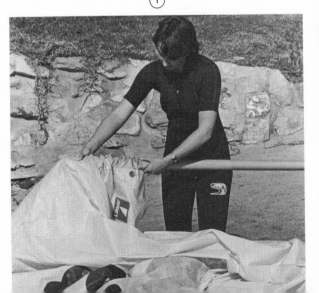

2. Prepare the mainsail by unfolding it and inserting the battens. With a rigged mast, ensure that halyards are free and clear and that the forestay is not tangled around the mast or other rigging.

3. Ensure that the boat is pointing head to wind, then erect the mast by lifting it into its step and securing it. With rigged masts, the forestay is tensioned and secured to hold the mast in position. The sail is not secured until later.

② ③ ④

4. Attach the boom, mainsheet and any other gear related to mast or rigging. At this point, the sails are bent on and hoisted if the boat has a rigged mast.

5. Check the mast to see that it is correctly plumbed. This is particularly important with rigged masts where adjustable tension on the forestay allows considerable fore and aft movement. Check all halyards and other mast fittings.

6. Tension the mainsail along the boom by means of the outhaul secured through the clew. If other tensioning devices are fitted, they should be adjusted to ensure that the sail is correctly shaped.

7. Fit the sheets as necessary, with any additional running rigging, such as the boom vang or kicker.

8. Clip on the rudder and fit the bungs. Check that all fittings are well secured.

9. The boat is rigged and ready to sail.

⑦

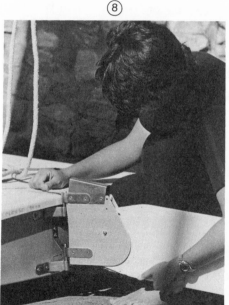
⑧

⑨

The wind that fills the sails

When the wind fills the sails of a boat, it sets up an aerodynamic force that drives the hull of the boat through the water. This is described in detail in the first booklet in this series *All About Sailboats*.

If the boat had no keel, the effect of the wind pressure on the sails would push the hull sideways across the water like a feather across a pond. By lowering a centreboard or keel beneath the hull, resistance is introduced, preventing the boat from being blown sideways.

Thus the boat is caught between two forces acting on each side directly opposite one another. Rather like an orange pip squeezed between thumb and finger, it has nowhere to go but forward.

The theoretical centre of the wind pressure in the sails is known as the **Centre of Effort** and the centre of the keel's resistance to the water is known as the **Centre of Lateral Resistance**. Between them they create the forward motion of the boat. The best performance is achieved when these two centres are located one over the other on a vertical line through the boat's hull and rig.

Achieving this is known as **balancing** the boat and is an important factor in a yacht's design. A boat which is well balanced sails easily without any need for correction, while a poorly balanced boat will constantly steer to one side, thus needing helm correction, a factor which greatly inhibits her performance.

The balance of the rig can be adjusted in a process known as 'tuning'. A well balanced boat is a joy to sail while an unbalanced craft will require constant adjustment and a lot of effort in handling, even in moderate conditions. In hard conditions she may well become unmanageable.

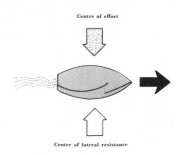

Centre of effort

Centre of lateral resistance

Handling the controls

There are two principal controls on a sailboat—the tiller, which controls the steering, and the sheets which control the sails. For the most part they work together and any adjustment to the helm requires adjustment of the sails. In most boats, the skipper handles the tiller and the crew handle the sheets, so successful sailing is obviously a team effort. This is particularly the case with sailboat racing.

In addition to controlling the setting of the mainsail, the main sheet is also the safety valve of the boat. When she heels too far and is in risk of a capsize, the main sheet is eased to relieve the pressure in the mainsail and bring her back to the upright.

Small, single-handed boats such as the Laser require skilled handling, for the skipper must handle both controls himself. Larger boats carry more sail but usually have more crew. The size of the crew on a performance boat is dictated by the number of sheets to be handled, although in large craft the size and weight of the gear often requires extra crewmen. An International 12 metre, for example, has only the same number of basic controls as a 480, but carries a crew of eleven or twelve instead of just two.

As a general rule, the skipper sits on the high or windward side and helm orders are related to this situation. **Up helm** means the tiller is pulled to the windward side and the boat's head swings away from the wind. **Down helm** means the tiller is pushed down to the lee side and the boat's head turns into the wind. **On sheets** is the term given to pulling the sails tighter and **ease sheets** the term for slacking them out. If they are eased too far, the sails will begin to collapse along the luff or front edge and the boat will slow down. The technical term for this condition is **luffing**, and it plays a great part in good sailing.

To obtain the best setting and therefore the best performance from the sails, the procedure is as follows:

1. Settle the boat on the required course.
2. 'Ease sheets' until the sails begin to luff.
3. 'On sheets' until any sign of luffing has ceased.

The sails are now set in their optimum position.

The boat and the wind

There are a number of terms used to describe the boat's relationship with the wind and as they are widely used in sailing, it is important to mention them here. Most are traditional and have their roots deep in maritime history. Although sailing has become very sophisticated with the advent of modern equipment, the traditional terms survive, adding colour to an already colourful sport.

Port side. This is the left side of the boat as you face forward. **Starboard side**. The right side of the boat as you face forward. **Windward side**. The side the wind is coming from. **Lee side**. The side opposite the wind. **Weather side**. Another term for windward side. **Port tack**. Sailing with the wind on the port side. **Starboard tack**. Sailing with the wind on the starboard side.

In small centreboarders, the skipper must handle all controls.

19

The sailing positions

Setting the sails at the correct angle to the wind is of extreme importance in sailing and indeed, much of the art of sailing revolves around sail setting. Since the boat's direction may vary and thus change the angle of the wind, the sails must be re-set to compensate. In other words, each time the boat changes course, the sails must be adjusted to retain their correct angle to the wind. When the wind is astern, the maximum drive is gained by spreading out the sails as much as possible to catch as much wind as possible. This is when spinnakers, bloopers and all kinds of extra sails are hoisted and spread out. By contrast, when the wind is ahead at a sharp angle on the bow, the sails are pulled in tight to create an aerofoil shape and induce forward drive to the boat.

Between these two extremes, the sails are set according to the direction of the wind. When the wind is on the beam, which is about halfway between right ahead and right astern, the sails are set about halfway between right in and right out. As the boat moves closer to the wind, the sails are brought in more, and as she moves away from the wind, the sails are eased out.

The major points of sailing and their correct sails settings are as follows:

1. **Close hauled**. This is the term given to sailing as close to the wind as possible and therefore with the sails pulled in as tight as possible to the boat.
2. **Close or 'shy' reaching**. As the wind broadens its angle to the bow, the sheets are eased a little (as far as they will go without luffing). This is termed close or shy reaching.
3. **Reaching**. This is sailing with the wind on the beam, or 90 degrees to the bow with the sails about halfway out. It is considered to be the most comfortable and the fastest point of sailing.
4. **Broad reaching**. When the wind is abaft the beam, but not right astern, the sails are well out but not right out. The boat is then said to be broad reaching.
5. **Running free**. With the wind right astern and the sails spread out as far as they will go, the boat is running free.

Close-hauled

Reaching

Running free

21

Basic sailing manoeuvres

To move from one sailing position to another, the boat has to make a sailing manoeuvre. There are two principal manoeuvres—sailing closer to the wind, and sailing farther away from the wind. Sailing closer to the wind is appropriately termed **Closing up**. Steering away from the wind is termed **Bearing away**.

As with all sailing manoeuvres, a change of course means re-setting the sails and, since the sails are close hauled when the wind is ahead and freed out when the wind is astern, it follows that a boat which manoeuvres closer to the wind—closes up—will need to bring her sails on tighter. Bearing away means bringing the wind farther astern and thus the sails will need to be freed out when this manoeuvre takes place.

1. **Closing up**. Assuming the boat to be off the wind, the first step is 'helm down'. As the boat moves closer to the wind, the sails will tend to luff. 'Sheets on' brings the sails in to the boat to prevent them luffing. The centreboard must be fully lowered to counteract sideways drift. Continuing this procedure will bring the boat up to the close hauled position.
2. **Bearing away**. The first manoeuvre is 'up helm'. As the boat bears away from the wind, 'ease sheets' to adjust the sails for offwind sailing. They should be eased as far as possible without allowing any luffing. Bearing away even further to the running free position means easing the sheets right out and pulling the centreboard right up.

Close up　　　　　　　　*Bear away*

The non-sailing zone

No sailboat can sail directly into the wind. To do so causes the wind to pass equally over both sides of the sail thus destroying the aerofoil shape and the drive. Most craft can sail to within 45 degrees of the wind, although some high performance sailboats can sail well inside that angle.

On an average, however, 45 degrees is accepted as the standard angle for sailing a yacht close hauled on either tack, which means that there is a non-sailing zone between tacks of 90 degrees. If a boat tries to sail inside this non-sailing zone, her sails will luff and eventually collapse and the boat will slow and eventually stop. This condition is known as **in irons** or **in stays** and is a condition that must be avoided since a boat in stays quickly loses steerage and gets out of control.

When sailing to windward, it is obviously important to sail the boat as close to the non-sailing zone as possible without slipping into it. This is done by setting the sails in the close hauled position and sailing the boat as close to the wind as possible without any sign of luffing appearing in the sails. As a rule, the luff of the headsail is the indicator since it is the first edge of any sail to cut the wind. The luff of the mainsail can be affected by backwind off the headsail, so this is not a good indicator.

As mentioned, some high-performance sailboats can point higher than the normal 45 degrees as a result of special tuning of their rigs and cut of their sails. It is obviously of great advantage for a racing boat to be able to point high, since it gives her far better ability to make progress to windward, and indeed, the pointing ability of a racing boat is one of her most important features.

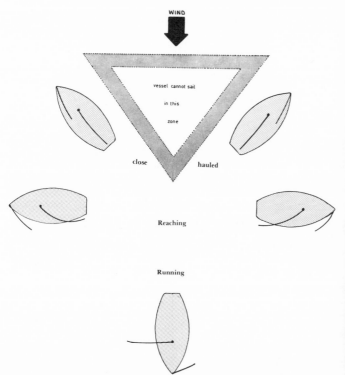

WIND

vessel cannot sail

in this

zone

close   hauled

Reaching

Running

Boat in irons. Bear away.

25

Going about (tacking)

In order to change from one tack to another, the boat must pass through the non-sailing zone.

1. The boat is brought up to the close hauled position ready to tack. 'Ready about!'

2. Helm down. 'Lee oh!' This is the order to the crew to switch jib sheets as the boat swings over onto the opposite tack.

3. 'Sheets on!' The helm is steadied as the sails are brought in and the boat sails off on the opposite tack.

Gybing

An alternative to changing tack by passing through the non-sailing zone is to swing the wind across the stern. It is known as gybing and is carried out as follows:

1. With the boat in the running free position; Up helm. 'Ready to gybe'.
2. 'Gybe oh!' The mainsail swings across the boat.
3. The new course is set on the opposite tack and the sheets adjusted as required.

Combining the skills

Having mastered the individual manoeuvres, we must now combine them in order to sail the boat in any required direction. A good exercise for this is to sail the boat right around the compass. The procedure is as follows:

1. Start with the boat in the close-hauled position. Let's say close-hauled on the port tack. 'Helm up, ease sheets!'
2. The boat bears away through the close reaching, reaching and broad reaching positions until she is running free on the port tack. 'Ready to Gybe!'

3. Gybe-oh! The boat is now running free on a starboard tack. 'Helm down, sheets on!'
4. The boat closes up through broad reaching, reaching and close reaching positions until she is close-hauled on the starboard tack. 'Ready about!'
5. Helm down. 'Lee-oh!' The boat sails up through the wind and goes about onto the port tack again.
6. Sheets on, helm amidships. The boat settles down close-hauled on the port tack having sailed through 360 degrees.

Tacking to windward

If a boat's destination lies within the non-sailing zone, she will not be able to sail directly towards it. In attempting to do so, her bow will come inside the non-sailing zone, she will luff, fall into stays and stop. Yet it is obviously important that she is able to sail to a windward destination, albeit not in a straight line. The procedure is known as 'tacking' or 'beating' to windward. It involves sailing the boat as close to the wind as possible—and therefore on the edge of the non-sailing zone—first on one tack and then the other. In this way she makes a zigzag across the non-sailing zone, gradually working closer and closer to her windward destination. The procedure is as follows:

1. Sheet on hard and bring the boat up to the close hauled position.
2. While sailing in this position, constantly try to point higher, but bear away the moment the headsail begins to luff. This will ensure that the boat is making the best progress up wind that is possible in the circumstances.

3. When the destination is on the beam, go about onto the other tack and repeat the procedure.
4. Repeat the tacking manoeuvre each time the destination is abeam.

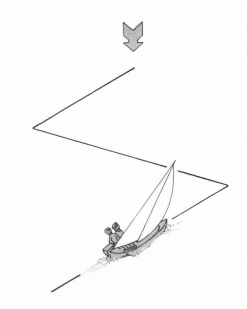

Leeway and the Centreboard

Yachts have fixed keels and therefore have no ability to change the underwater surface area as wind conditions change. But centreboarders have a retractable keel and this can be used to advantage when sailing conditions vary.

On a downwind run, for example, when there is no need for a keel, the centreboard is pulled up to reduce the underwater drag. With the boat close hauled and the maximum lateral resistance required, the centreboard is lowered to its fullest extent. In between these two extremes the centreboard is adjusted according to the sailing position at the time.

1. Close hauled. Centreboard right down.
2. Reaching. Centreboard half up.
3. Running. Centreboard right up.

Sailing off a beach (Offshore wind)

Sailing off a beach is easy if the wind is offshore or across the beach. The boat is pushed clear, the sails sheeted on as required, the rudder and centreboard lowered and the boat sailed straight out.

1. Hold the boat head to wind with the sheets free so that she remains static, and prepare all gear for sailing off.
2. Push her clear of the beach and jump aboard.
3. Rudder down, centreboard down. 'Sheets on!' Set course and adjust sheets as required.

Sailing off a beach (Onshore wind)

The problems of getting off a beach become more acute with an onshore wind. Since the boat must be sailed to windward, the centreboard must be fully lowered and this is not always possible until the boat is into deep water. As a result she is often blown back on the beach before the sheets are on, the centreboard lowered and the boat is under way. The manoeuvre requires a fair amount of dexterity and a lot of frustrating practice before it can be perfected. The basic manoeuvres are as follows:

1. Ensure that the boat is head to wind and well prepared before shoving off.
2. A good hard push will send her out into deep water. Scramble aboard over the transom and get the sheets on and the centreboard down as soon as possible.
3. Tiller hard up to bear away from the wind. Sheets on and centreboard down. The boat is in the close hauled position ready to tack away from the beach.

Sailing onto a beach

The manoeuvres used for sailing onto a beach are similar to those used for sailing off. The problems, too, are much the same. If the wind is onshore or across the beach, the boat is simply sailed in with the centreboard raised or partly raised.

If the wind is off the beach, then she must be tacked in. This requires the centreboard to be fully lowered which creates problems as the boat sails closer to the beach and into shallow water. Indeed, it becomes quite impossible in the final stages of sailing onto the beach.

One way of overcoming the problem is to tack the boat in until the water shallows, then bear away a little to get up speed, and throw her hard up into the wind, raising the centreboard at the same time. Her momentum should carry her ashore.

When sailing in on a reach or run, the boat may pick up considerable speed and risk damaging her bottom as she grounds on the beach. It is a good practice to 'round out' at the last moment to reduce speed and lessen the impact. This is done by freeing all sheets and pushing the helm hard down just as she is about to ground. The boat heads up into the wind, her speed washes off and she broadsides gently onto the beach.

Perfect landing. Centreboard up, boat rounded out head to wind before hitting the beach.

Capsize

No matter how good a sailor you are, sooner or later you will be involved in a capsize. Providing the boat is properly fitted with buoyancy, she will remain afloat and providing you are wearing a life-jacket, there is no risk of drowning. There is no need to panic and indeed that is the worst thing you can do, for panic is quickly communicated to others and creates worse problems.

Most centreboarders are relatively easy to right even if they are totally upside down, providing the centreboard is secured. If it cannot be extended from the bottom of the hull or, even worse, if it is not secured and floats away, then righting the boat will be very difficult. The moral is to ensure that the centreboard, like all loose gear in the boat, is well secured and cannot be lost in the event of a capsize.

If the boat cannot be righted or bailed out after she has been righted, then stay with her until help can be summoned. Attempting to swim ashore, even if it appears within swimming distance, can be disasterous. Unexpected tidal currents, exhaustion, hypothermia or simply misjudgement of the distance can prove fatal.

1. Catamarans are difficult boats to right and require special techniques for recovery when capsized.
2. Before attempting to right the boat, free all sheets and ensure that the centreboard is fully extended.

3. Swim round to the centreboard, grasp it and use your body weight to start righting the boat. Apply pressure steadily along the length of the board to avoid breaking it.
4. Grasp the gunwale, as soon as it is within reach, for extra leverage.
5. With the sheets free, the boat will lie quietly while you clamber aboard. If there is sufficient crew, one man should lie in the water at the bow holding the boat head to wind.
6. Bail out the boat, sort out the gear, and get her sailing again. If she cannot be bailed, or there is something wrong, sail or paddle to the nearest beach.

Sailing rules of the road

Although the principal rules of the road for sailboats are international, some harbours and waterways have special rules related to navigation, particularly where big freighters, ferries and similar commercial or naval craft are concerned. It is important, therefore, to know the rules of the waterway in which you are sailing. Similarly, there are special rules for yachts and other sailboats engaged in racing which, although they do not give any special right of way as far as other craft are concern, apply specific rules to all craft engaged in a race.

The three principal international rules relating to sail craft are as follows:
1. When two sailboats are on opposite tacks, the boat on the port tack must give way to the boat on the starboard tack. Wherever possible, the boat that gives way must avoid crossing ahead of the other sailboat.

2. When both sailboats are on the same tack, the windward boat (i.e. the one which gets the wind first) must give way to the leeward boat.

3. A sailboat overtaking any other boat (even a power boat) must keep clear of the boat she is overtaking.

Other rules which apply to sailboats are as follows:

- Power boats give way to sail boats except, as described in rule 3 above, when the sailboat is overtaking the power boat.

- Sailboats, like all other boats, must give way to vessels towing, hampered or disabled.

- When crossing designated traffic zones, sailboats must cross as nearly as possible at right angles to the flow of traffic.

- Although not a written rule, it is an accepted courtesy that boats not engaged in racing keep clear of racing craft.

Balancing the boat

The pressure of wind on the large surface area of a boat's sails makes her very unstable, and without some form of counterbalance she will most certainly capsize.

Apart from the risk of capsize, the boat's performance deteriorates the farther she heels. Heeling reduces the effective depth of the keel or centreboard in the water, allowing the boat to skid sideways across the surface. Similarly, a heeled mast presents a less effective sail surface to the wind and much useful power is lost as the wind slips off the angled sail.

The more upright a boat sails, the better her performance, so steps are taken with all types of sailcraft to minimise the heel as much as possible. The method used will, of course, vary with the type of craft.

Keel yachts have a counterbalancing weight fitted to the bottom of the keel in the form of ballast. The more the yacht is heeled, the more the keel is tilted upwards and the greater its righting effect pulling the boat back upright. Since the pressure in the sails becomes less as the yacht heels and the righting effect more, it is easy to see why a ballast keel yacht is a very stable type of boat and virtually non-capsizeable under normal sailing conditions.

Sailing dinghies, catamarans and sailboards have no ballast and are very vulnerable to both heeling and capsize. They rely on the counterbalancing effect of crew body-weight to keep them upright. The crew may apply righting lever by sitting on the windward gunwale or sliding out on boards or 'wings' to carry their weight out to windward as far as possible. On high performance racing craft the crew may swing out in a trapeze. This is a wire sling attached to the top of the mast to apply maximum leverage against the boat's heel.

Trapezing is a fine sailing skill, for as the boat flies through varying gusts and wind shifts, the trapeze man (or men) must move his weight quickly but smoothly to counteract the varying degrees of pressure in the sail. Some of the finest and most spectacular sailing can be seen when Australian 18-foot skiffs are racing. These remarkable craft reach speeds of 20 knots with a team of three or four out in trapezes.

Emergency

Providing the boat is well-found and fitted with adequate buoyancy, and providing the crew are wearing the correct support gear, there are few serious emergencies that can arise in the course of sailing small boats. With an approved life-jacket it is impossible to drown even if, for some reason, you are unconscious. Correctly designed jackets not only support an unconscious person with his head above water, but will turn him over onto his back if he is lying face down in the water.

The buoyancy in the boat is also important. It must be sufficient to support the boat when waterlogged, together with its gear and occupants. It must keep the gunwales above the water or bailing out will be impossible, particularly in choppy seas. If the boat cannot be bailed, she must be sailed or paddled to the nearest beach, but needless to say, a boat that is totally awash is very hard to move and sluggish to respond to any helm movements.

She will also be at the mercy of tidal currents and this must be taken into consideration when deciding where to beach her. So that she can be handled when full of water, the buoyancy must be distributed to keep her afloat on an even keel. Bailing out a boat with her transom low in the water is virtually impossible no matter how high out of the water the rest of the hull is. Similarly, if one gunwale or the other is low, water will pour aboard as fast as it is bailed out.

If all else fails and you cannot get the boat to shore, she must be used as a survival platform to which you can cling until help arrives. A basic maxim with all maritime emergencies of this nature is to **stay with the boat**. The shore can appear temptingly close, but apart from the fact that it is always farther away than it appears, there are many dangerous, even fatal, unknowns in the stretch of water between the boat and the shore.

An unexpected current can sweep you quickly away from both boat and shore. Cramp or exhaustion may move in before you are halfway, and in warm waters there may be the risk of sharks or other predators. Most of these risks can be reduced, if not eliminated, by staying with the boat. Providing the boat is above water and you can sit in or on it, you should have every chance of survival.

The one danger that cannot be eliminated is hypothermia. This is the weakening of the body system caused by prolonged cold. It is obviously more of a risk in colder climates, but should not be ignored, even in warm waters. A saturated body exposed to a cool wind can rapidly loose temperature in any condition. The right clothing is the best insurance against hypothermia (see earlier in this book).

Small craft are happily free of most of the other maritime dangers which plague larger craft. Fire is almost unknown and grounding or stranding can usually be rectified by lifting the centreboard or, at worst, getting out and shoving the boat into deeper water. Dismasting is also a fairly moderate emergency since, if you cannot re-rig the mast or it is broken, you can paddle home and fix it later!

Man overboard!

The procedure for recovering a man overboard varies according to the size of boat concerned and the conditions that exist at the time. Picking up a man in the open sea requires a totally different approach to picking up a man from a river or lake. Since there is no space here to cover all methods, and since this booklet is orientated mainly towards small craft, the procedure described is the basic system used with small craft recovering a man overboard in reasonably sheltered waters.

1. As soon as the man is overboard, bear away easily. If you turn too sharply the boat may run down the man in the water.
2. Sweep round into an easy gybe, then position the boat on a reach back, aiming at a point a little downwind of the man in the water.
3. Round up into the wind, let fly the sheets and steer to run alongside the man overboard.
4. Judging the speed to round up and lose way so that the boat stops when she is alongside the man in the water requires a lot of practice.

If the boat is travelling too fast, the dead weight of the man in the water will tear him from your grasp.

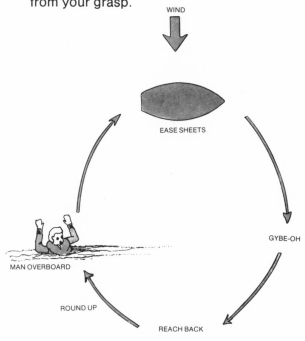

WIND

EASE SHEETS

GYBE-OH

MAN OVERBOARD

ROUND UP

REACH BACK

Heaving-to

By heaving-to, the boat can be stopped and then held in almost any required position for any length of time. It is a practice widely used in the days of the old windjammers, but not commonly used nowadays although it is just as effective with yachts. The windjammers backed their upper sails against their lower sails to cancel out the wind effect. Yachts back the headsail against the mainsail.

Although the boat does not remain exactly in the one spot, she lies comfortably at an angle to the wind, making very slight leeward movement. Heaving-to can be used for a number of purposes, not least of which is as a man overboard drill. It stops the boat and holds her in an upwind position, making recovery of a man overboard—providing he can swim—relatively easy.

The procedure for heaving-to is as follows:

1. Put the helm down and swing the boat up into the wind. Bring the sheets hard on.
2. Let her swing right up into and across the wind as though making a tack, but do not touch the sheets.
3. As she pays off on the opposite tack, the jib will be **backed** as the sheets have not been changed over.
4. Secure the helm hard down. The effect of the main and helm attempting to bring the boat back into the wind will be cancelled out by the backed jib attempting to push her off the wind. The boat will stop and settle down with her bow slightly off the wind.

Anchors and anchoring

Apart from being a useful piece of equipment when you wish to 'park' the boat for an overnight stop in a quiet bay, the anchor is a very important part of the boat's safety gear. When a problem arises, the anchor is the only factor which can prevent the boat from drifting into danger. The anchor will hold the boat in one position until either the problem is resolved or help arrives.

The most popular types of anchors are those which hold well when dropped to the sea bed and which stow easily when brought aboard. The best holding anchor of all, the **Admiralty** anchor, is cumbersome to stow, so despite its good qualities in use, it is rarely found aboard small craft. The **Plough** (or **CQR**) and the **Danforth** are the two most popular anchors for small craft. They are both good holding anchors and yet can both be stowed fairly easily aboard even small keel yachts.

The **anchor warp** is just as important as the anchor itself. It is a long length of laid nylon line with a few metres of chain securing it to the anchor. The importance of the warp lies in its

shock-absorbing qualities which prevent the anchor from being plucked out of the bottom. The warp must be paid out for some length—say around five times the depth of the water—so that it hangs in a 'bight' between the anchor and the boat. As the boat rides back on the anchor, this bight absorbs the strain which would otherwise pull the anchor out of the sea bed. Carrying sufficient warp is obviously as important as carrying the correct type of anchor.

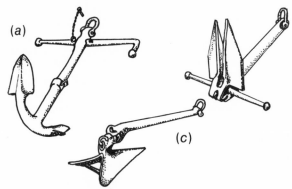

(a) Admiralty anchor (b) Danforth anchor (c) Plough (CQR) anchor

Anchoring

The procedure for coming to an anchor under sail is as follows:

1. Reduce sail by taking down the jib as the boat approaches the anchorage on a reach.
2. Round up into the wind from a position just downwind of the anchoring spot and let fly the main sheets. It is not wise to drop the sail at this stage in case the anchor does not hold and the exercise has to be aborted.
3. The speed of the boat must be judged so that when she rounds up and loses way, she comes to a stop some way to windward of the required anchoring spot. At this point drop the anchor and ensure that the main sheets are completely free, for the boat will now start to fall back. Keep a slight tension on the anchor warp to ensure that her head does not pay off too far.
4. When the boat has brought up to the anchor, indicated by the feel of the warp and also the fact that she has swung up head to wind, drop the mainsail. Adjust the warp for the correct length required, and snub up on the bollard or mooring cleat.

Racing

Almost everyone who owns a sailboat gets involved in racing at some time. It may just be social racing with a small club, or it may be hot-shot racing with performance craft. Either way there are many benefits to be obtained, for racing develops the basic sailing skills to a fine degree. Whether you are just a weekend sailor looking to improve your techniques, or a skilled performer looking to add more trophies to your collection, racing provides the means.

One-design class racing

One-design racing is the most demanding of all. In this aspect of the sport, all the boats, their rigs and sails are identical, often checked by computer to ensure that no one boat gains any advantage over another. So the difference between the boats is purely the skipper and crew, and this creates very intense competitive racing. Small craft such as Lasers fall into one-design class category, while J24s and Etchells 22s are one-design boats in the keel yacht classification.

Level rating class racing

Sometimes called the 'ton' classes, the qualifications for these categories in racing yachts is the result of a complex configuration of the boat's dimensions. This type of class provides boat-for-boat racing in offshore waters which is as close to one-design class racing as you can get without building every boat in the same mould.

Handicap racing

Most offshore and all non-class yachts race on a handicap basis in which the faster boats are penalised by a time factor. With crack ocean racing yachts, the handicap factor is worked out from the boat's dimensions, much as with level rating yachts. The time correction factor, as it is called, is then applied to the time taken to complete a race to arrive at a corrected time on which the race results are based.

For more detail on racing of all types of sailboats, see No. 5 in this series of booklets, *Yacht Racing for Beginners*.

Spinnakers

The spinnaker is known as an 'extra' sail since it is not part of the boat's basic rig. It can only be used when the boat is off the wind, most spinnakers being used for broad reaching or running free. Unlike the headsail and mainsail, the spinnaker is a 'free flying' sail in that it is not secured along any edge, but flies free from each of its three corners. This, plus the fact that it is a very full cut sail, makes it more difficult to set and fly than other sails.

Spinnakers are cut in different styles, ranging from flat cut spinnakers which are little more than a free flying genoa jib, to giant balloon or parachute spinnakers which fill with wind and belly out, creating enormous drive pressures. The type of cut is seen by the panels of the sail which are usually brightly coloured and thus create a colourful pattern when the sail is flying.

Setting the spinnaker

A spinnaker is secured only at the corners and is a difficult sail to set and fly. It requires a

spinnaker pole to hold out the tack of the sail, and this pole is usually carried on deck until required, then hoisted into position by a **topping lift** and secured by a **downhaul**. Adjustment of these two ropes permits the pole to be raised and lowered vertically. Fore and aft movement is controlled by a **brace** or **guy**. The inner end of the pole is secured to the mast and the outer end supports the tack of the sail.

The spinnaker is either hoisted behind the headsail, or stoppered up with wool hanks so that it looks like a long sausage. This is to prevent the sail from filling with wind until it is fully hoisted. A flogging spinnaker, full of wind and only half hoisted, can behave like a beserk wild animal and cause untold damage to the boat and crew before it is brought under control. If the sail is hoisted behind the headsail, secured at the top of the mast and then sheeted on as the headsail is dropped, it will behave rationally. Similarly, a stoppered spinnaker can be kept under control until it is hoisted and secured. It is then broken out by pulling on the sheet.

Trailering

Different states have different trailer regulations, but generally speaking, the weight of the trailer and its load must not be more than the weight of the car, and over a certain weight, special hitches and over-rider brakes are required. It is obviously important to check the regulations in your area before even buying the boat or you may find that you will have to buy a new car which can legally tow the boat.

However, the law says nothing (as a rule) about how you load your trailer, and incorrect weight distribution can cause some of the most severe problems when towing a boat. For example, too much weight at the front of the trailer will put a great deal of stress on the car structure. Too much weight aft may cause the trailer to slew around, throw the car out of control and possibly cause an accident.

The load on the hitch should give moderate downwards pressure. With most medium-sized craft that means you can lift the trailer arm without getting a hernia, but not without a little effort. Correct balance of the rig behind the car makes towing much easier and safer and reduces wear and tear on the car and the trailer, to say nothing, of course, of the owner!

Launching and retrieving

Ramps are usually very busy on sailing days, so it is good practice to have the boat all ready to drop off the trailer when your turn comes to launch. You will not make yourself popular if you rig the boat as she sits on the ramp. Most ramps have an area designated for preparing the boat, but even if you do not use this, utilise your time in the queue getting the boat ready so that when you are next on the ramp, the boat will be launched and clear in a matter of seconds.

A word of warning, however. If you decide to rig the boat on the trailer—and there is nothing wrong with this—make absolutely sure that there are no overhead obstructions on the way to the ramp which will foul the mast and rigging. Apart from damaging the gear on overhanging tree branches, there is a risk at some ramps of snarling high tension power cables, and when an aluminium mast hits high power cables, a serious accident will almost certainly result.

When retrieving the boat, the wind or tide will sometimes swing her stern to one side so that it is difficult to winch her up on the trailer. A line run ashore from the transom to a person on the bank upwind of the ramp will give all the control necessary and make retrieving simple even in blustery conditions.

Launching small boats can be done anywhere there are a few helpers.

Advanced sailing manoeuvres

The test of a proficient boat handler comes not in the open water, but when manoeuvring in tight corners such as through moorings, alongside a jetty or into a marina. Limitations of manoeuvring room and wind direction call for a high degree of expertise.

Sailing onto a mooring

All manoeuvring with a sailboat, no matter what size, is controlled by wind direction. The boat cannot sail in the non-sailing zone under any circumstances, so that zone is a good area in which to stall her, take off speed and bring her to a stop. And since it is at times necessary to use such manoeuvres, the non-sailing zone can be usefully employed.

When sailing onto a mooring the procedure is as follows:

1. Manoeuvre the boat so that she is sailing towards the mooring on a beam reach.
2. Bear away slightly and ease sheets so that she points a little downwind of the mooring.
3. When directly downwind of the mooring buoy, round her hard up into the wind and let the sheets fly.
4. As the speed comes off the boat, steer directly towards the mooring buoy. If the manoeuvre has been correctly executed, the boat should be virtually stopped as the buoy is reached.

Sailing up to a jetty

If there is good sea room around the jetty this manoeuvre is only a little more difficult than sailing onto a mooring. The main problem is that often there is no room to overshoot, and misjudging the amount of distance required to round up head to wind and stop the boat, can lead to the boat hitting the jetty.

Wind across the jetty

Approach from the lee side, sailing along the jetty at the required distance off, then round up head to wind so that the boat coasts up to the jetty. This is best practiced at the end of the jetty where there is room to overshoot if need be.

Wind along jetty

Sail directly towards the jetty, then round up head to wind when close in, easing the boat gently towards the jetty as the speed comes off.

Sailing off a jetty

Once again, different wind direction require different manoeuvres. The basic procedures are as follows:

Wind across jetty

Keep the sheets very loose until ready to let go. Sheet on the headsail. This will pull her bow away from the jetty. Sheet on the mainsail and sail away.

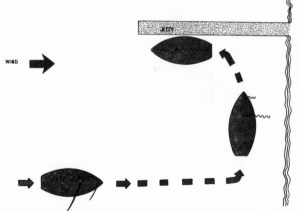

Wind along jetty

The boat must be swung head to wind or the sails cannot be hoisted. Keep the mainsheet completely free. Back the headsail to push her bow away from the jetty. When she is clear, lee-oh the headsail and take on both sails. The boat will sail away.

Sailing out of a marina berth

Sailing in and out of a marina berth or dock requires very advanced sailing techniques and indeed, there are times when such manoeuvres are just not possible as the wind is totally in the wrong quarter. However, since the boat must be manoeuvred somehow or other, and assuming no motor is available, the procedures for getting out of a dock are as follows:

Wind ahead

When the sails have been hoisted, keep the sheets totally free. Hand the boat backwards out of the dock until clear. Back the headsail to turn her bow in the required direction, then lee-oh the headsail and sheet on both sails to get her sailing.

Wind astern

It is not possible to hoist the sails with the wind astern, so the boat must be handed backwards out of the berth and allowed to swing across the end of the dock. It may be possible to hoist the sails in this position, but if not she must be backed into the dock and the procedure followed for sailing out with the wind ahead.

Wind across the dock

If the sails can be hoisted in this position, hoist the main with the sheets free. Gradually take on the sheets after letting go the mooring lines until the boat moves out of the berth.

Sailing into a marina berth

Once again, handing the boat and even using lines may be necessary depending on the wind conditions.

Wind blowing out of the dock

Sail the boat easily on a reach until opposite the dock, adjusting her speed by adjusting the sheets (probably main only). Round up head to wind, sheets free and steer into the dock.

Wind blowing into dock

Sail the boat on a reach towards the dock entrance. When some way off, drop all sails completely and allow her forward way to carry her into the berth.

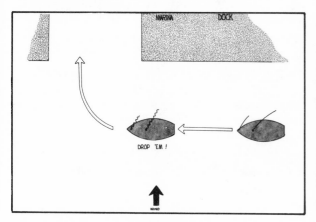

Wind blowing across the dock

Tack or run towards the dock entrance, then steer her into the berth, freeing all sheets to control her forward speed.

Some common sailors' knots

Figure-of-eight knot. *Used to prevent sheets running out through a sheeting block or eye. Turn the end of the rope back over its own standing part, then under it, back up and down through the loop thus created.* ▶

▲ **Reef knot.** *Used for joining two ends of rope of equal size. Form a loop with the left hand end without crossing the rope. Pass the right hand end up through the loop, around the back of the two left hand ropes and back down through the loop.*

Single sheet bend. *Used for joining two ends* ▲ *of rope of unequal thickness. Form a loop in the end of the thicker rope without crossing it over itself. Pass the end of the smaller rope up through this loop, around the back of both parts of thicker rope, around the front, and back under itself.*

Bowline. *Used for forming a loop that will not slip. Make the loop the required size. Twist the standing part for form a small loop with the standing part* **under**. *Pass the end of the rope up through this loop, around the back of the standing part and back down through the small loop.*

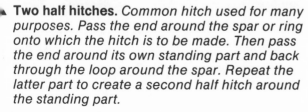

Two half hitches. *Common hitch used for many purposes. Pass the end around the spar or ring onto which the hitch is to be made. Then pass the end around its own standing part and back through the loop around the spar. Repeat the latter part to create a second half hitch around the standing part.*

Clove hitch. *Used for tying up boats to rings or rails. Pass the end of the rope around the rail, cross it over itself and pass it around again. Bring the end back through the loop thus formed.*

61

Glossary

Abaft	Behind
Abeam	At right angles to the boat's heading
Adrift	Drifting across the water
Aft	Behind
Ahead	Forward. In front
Ahull	Adrift without sails
Aloft	Up in the rigging
Anchor	Used to secure the boat to the sea bed
Astern	Behind
Backstay	Standing rigging supporting mast from aft
Ballast	Weight placed in keel to stabilise boat
Beam	Maximum cross measurement of the hull. See **abeam**
Bear away	Steer away from the wind
Beating	Tacking to windward
Bend	Type of knot
Block	A pulley—block and tackles
Boathook	Long pole with hook for picking up moorings
Boltrope	Rope sewn into edge of sail
Boom	The spar which carries the foot of the mainsail
Bow	'Sharp end' of the boat
Bowline	Nautical knot
Buoyancy	Flotation material fitted to support swamped boat
Cap	Top of the mast
Carry away	Break
Cast off	Let go
Catamaran	Boat with twin hulls
Chainplates	Hull fittings to which shrouds are secured
Cleat	Fitting for securing rope
Close-hauled	Sailing as close to the wind as possible
Crosstrees	Spars which stick out from mast to spread shrouds
Downhaul	Rope or tackle used to secure spars to deck

Term	Definition	Term	Definition
Ease-sheets	Order to slack away sheets	Helm	The device which steers the boat
Figure of eight	Knot used for stoppering sheets	Hoist	Pull up
		Jib	Small headsail
Foot	Bottom edge of a sail	Keel	Downward extension of the hull that prevents drift
Forward	Up front		
Foul	Tangle or obstruction		
Genoa	A large headsail which overlaps the mainsail	Kicking strap	Type of downhaul used to control the boom
Gunwale	The outer edge of the deck	Knot	Terms used to describe a bend or hitch. Also one nautical mile per hour
Gybe	Changing tack with the wind astern		
Hanks	Clips securing the headsail to the forestay	Lee	The area away from the wind
Hatch	Opening in the deck allowing access to the hull	Lee-oh	Order given to change jib sheets when tacking
		Leech	Back edge of the sail
Headsail	Sail carried forward of the mast on the forestay	Luff	Front edge of the sail
		Luffing	Flutter along the luff indicating sail is collapsing
Heave-to	Holding the boat stationary in one position	Mainsail	Sail carried on the after side of the main mast
Heel	The lean of the boat under wind pressure	Mooring	Permanent attachment to the sea bed

Outhaul	Tackle used to tension the foot of a sail	Stays	Standing rigging supporting the mast fore and aft
Plane	To skid across the surface of the water	Spars	Boom, spreaders, gaff and similar parts of the rig
Port	Left side of the boat facing forward	Spinnaker	Free flying sail used for downwind running
Port tack	Sailing with the wind on the port side	Spreaders	See **crosstrees**
Quarter	The after corner of the hull	Starboard	Right hand side of the boat facing forward
Reef	Reducing sail in heavy weather	Starboard tack	Sailing with the wind on the starboard side
Reef knot	A bend used to join two pieces of rope	Stem	Bow or front edge of the hull
Rigging	Wires and ropes used aboard a boat	Stern	Transom or after end of the hull
Running	Sailing with the wind astern. 'Running Free'	Tackle	Ropes and blocks used for hauling gear
Shackle	Metal joining piece used widely on small craft	Tell tales	Ribbons or wool used to indicate wind direction
Sheet	Rope to control a sail	Transom	The boat's stern
Shoal	Shallow area	Trapeze	A sling secured by wire to the top of the mast
Shrouds	Standing rigging supporting the mast on either side	Traveller	The securing gear for the mainsheet